The Critical Idiom

General Editor: JOHN D. JUMP

---

26 The Sonnet

In the same series

The Sonnet / *John Fuller*

Methuen & Co Ltd

First published 1972
by Methuen & Co Ltd
11 New Fetter Lane London EC4
© *1972 John Fuller*
Printed in Great Britain
by Cox & Wyman Ltd, Fakenham, Norfolk

SBN 416 65680 3 Hardback
SBN 416 65690 0 Paperback

Distributed in the U.S.A. by
HARPER & ROW PUBLISHERS, INC.
BARNES & NOBLE IMPORT DIVISION

73 - 152 332

Contents

General Editor's Preface

This volume is one of a series of short studies, each dealing with a single key item, or a group of two or three key items, in our critical vocabulary. The purpose of the series differs from that served by the standard glossaries of literary terms. Many terms are adequately defined for the needs of students by the brief entries in these glossaries, and such terms will not be the subjects of studies in the present series. But there are other terms which cannot be made familiar by means of compact definitions. Students need to grow accustomed to them through simple and straightforward but reasonably full discussions of them. The purpose of this series is to provide such discussions.

Some of the terms in question refer to literary movements (e.g. 'Romanticism', 'Aestheticism', etc.), others to literary kinds (e.g. 'Comedy', 'Epic', etc.), and still others to stylistic features (e.g. 'Irony', 'The Conceit', etc.). Because of this diversity of subject-matter, no attempt has been made to impose a uniform pattern upon the studies. But all authors have tried to provide as full illustrative quotation as possible, to make reference whenever appropriate to more than one literature, and to compose their studies in such a way as to guide readers towards the short bibliographies in which they have made suggestions for further reading.

John D. Jump

University of Manchester

I

The Italian Sonnet

The sonnet has a good claim to be one of the oldest and most useful verse forms in English. Like the engraving or the string quartet it provides simple yet flexible means to a classic artistic end: the expression of as much gravity, substance and lyrical beauty as a deceptively modest form can bear. The form is a minor one, but capable of the greatest things and, like all such forms which potential variety keeps alive, must jealously preserve its true lineaments and their rules.

Thus it is the Italian (or Petrarchan) sonnet which is the legitimate form, for it alone recognizes that peculiar imbalance of parts which is its salient characteristic. The English sonnet, which will be discussed in the next chapter, does something rather different with the form which is not quite as interesting or as subtle. Certain other freak varieties, discussed in the third chapter, pay tribute only to the powerful echoes of the form that perversions of it essentially deny. Indeed, at all periods, fascination with the idea of the sonnet has tended to take precedence over its legitimate use. There are a multitude of experiments adapting its rhyme-schemes to the poet's particular talents, and its history is littered with strokes of brilliant licence and the drudgery of persistent misunderstanding.

The first sonnets were written by Giacomo da Lentino, a Sicilian lawyer at the court of Frederick II, in about 1230 or 1240, and the Italian form used in the following century by Cavalcanti, Dante and Petrarch was very soon established. The practice of these early sonneteers provides us with the sonnet's form and its terminology. The rhyme-scheme and arrangement of lines is as follows:

First quatrain, or quadernario
{ a
b
b
a

Octave, or Piedi: closed rhyme (rima chiusa)

Second quatrain
{ a
b
b
a

Turn, or volta

First tercet, or terzetto
{ c
d
e

Sestet, or Volte: interlaced rhyme (rima incatenata)

Second tercet
{ c
d
e

The essence of the sonnet's form is the unequal relationship between octave and sestet. This relationship is of far greater significance than the fact that there are fourteen lines in the sonnet, for not every quatorzain is a sonnet, whereas the structural imbalance of parts preserved in, say, Hopkins's curtal sonnet (see p. 29) at least acknowledges the characteristic argument or feeling of the form. This bipartite structure is one of observation and conclusion, or statement and counter-statement. The turn after the octave, sometimes signalled by a white line in the text, is a shift of thought or feeling which develops the subject of the sonnet by surprise or conviction to its conclusion.

Italian theoreticians have been keen to stress the logical basis of the form, that the first quatrain states a proposition and the second proves it, that the first tercet confirms it and the second draws the conclusion. The sonnet's form has even been linked to the syllogism (Ceva, *Scelta di Sonetti*, Turin, 1735, p. 42), but this is no more convincing than other theories of its origin, such as in the Greek choral ode (strophe, antistrophe, epode, antepode), in 'the antithetic *Parallelisms* of *Scriptural Poetry*' (Lofft, p. xxxiii) or in the musical gamut (Lofft, pp. v ff.). In fact, the sonnet's origins support the idea that the bipartite form is the result of a prosodic sleight-of-hand. The eight lines of closed rhyme produce a certain kind of musical pace which demands repetition. Any expectation of stanzaic continuation is, however, violated by the six lines of interlaced rhyme which follow: the sestet is more tightly organized, and briefer, than the octave and so urges the sonnet to a decisive conclusion. The point is sharply put by Christopher Pilling in the sestet of a sonnet itself: 'this sonnet's nucleus/Leaps from octet to sestet and does not know/There are less lines to go than have been unreeled' (*Snakes and Girls*, Leeds, 1970, p. 42). This tension, implicit in the sestet by virtue of its being shorter, is preserved in a number of legitimate varieties of sestet, that is to say those which acknowledge the unity of the rhyme scheme, support the organization in tercets and do not too closely resemble the octave in structure. Some of these are as follows:

Type 1	Type 2	Type 3	Type 4	Type 5		
c	c	c	c	c	c	c
d	d	d	d	c	c	c
e	c	e	e	d	d	d
c	d	d	c	e	c	e
d	c	c	e	d	c	e
e	d	e	d	e	d	d

Type 1	Type 2	Type 3	Type 4	Type 5
Interlaced rhyme	Open rhyme (rima alternata)			French type

It will be evident that the possible varieties of sestet are very great (Equicola, and most Italian prosodists indeed, say that any order may be followed in the sestet), but these are among the most popular: of Petrarch's 317, for instance, 116 are of type 1, 107 are of type 2 and 67 type 3; of Camões's 196, 102 are type 1 and 56 type 2. Types such as cdcdee move even further than the French type 5 from the two tercets necessary to the Italian sonnet: by employing a terminal rather than internal couplet, it is very close to the English sonnet. Some freak forms (e.g. cccddd), while preserving some of the principles of the Italian sestet, manage invariably to violate others. The classic types are 1 and 2, and it is worth noting that of the first known group of nineteen sonnets (fifteen by Lentino, and four by contemporaries) thirteen have type 1 sestets, and six type 2. The fifth type is sometimes known as the sonnet *Marotique* from the practice of the early French sonneteer Clément Marot. Here the important factor is the early position of the couplet.

However, to return to the sonnet as a whole, we find that the octaves of these original specimens are not in closed rhyme at all but in open rhyme (abababab). The closed rhyme of the established sonnet was introduced by the Tuscan poet Guitone d'Arezzo (1230–94). It will be objected therefore that those sonnets with type 2 sestets do not possess the necessary contrast of rhyme-scheme, but are entirely in open rhyme, suggesting division not into quatrains but into distichs. This may be partly true but, as Wilkins points out, there *is* in fact a tendency to division into quatrains in the octave (as there is also in the heroic octaves of Tasso and Ariosto), and the sense and punctuation in the type 2 sestet, which Wilkins considers the later, shows a tendency towards division into tercets. Clearly the type 1 sestet is the more satisfactory, however.

The open form of octave shows the likely origin of the sonnet in the *strambotto* in its normal Sicilian form – the eight-line *canzuna* sung by Sicilian peasants but not actually recorded until later than the time of Frederick II. Type 2 sestets hint a similar origin from the *strambotto*, but Wilkins believes that type 1 is earlier, and anyway the six-line *canzuna* is very rare. Wilkins follows Rajna in thinking the sestet simply a stroke of inspiration, and some critics (e.g. Praz) believe that this relationship between octave and sestet is due to a change of tune in the sonnet's original musical setting.

This opportunity for a change of tune may be taken in many different ways, though in nearly all of them the sestet provides some kind of consolidation of the material introduced in the octave. It 'supports the octave as the cup supports the acorn' (Lever, p. 7). A familiar example is Keats's 'On First Looking into Chapman's Homer'. Note how the type 2 sestet encourages the tendency in a great many English writers of Italian sonnets to organize the sestet in distichs rather than in tercets. This tendency is even to be found in Keats's octave:

> Much have I travelled in the realms of gold,
>   And many goodly states and kingdoms seen;
>   Round many western islands have I been
> Which bards in fealty to Apollo hold.
> Oft of one wide expanse had I been told
>   That deep-browed Homer ruled as his demesne;
>   Yet did I never breathe its pure serene
> Till I heard Chapman speak out loud and bold:
>
> Then felt I like some watcher of the skies
>   When a new planet swims into his ken;
> Or like stout Cortez when with eagle eyes
>   He stared at the Pacific, and all his men
> Looked at each other with a wild surmise –
>   Silent, upon a peak in Darien.

The beauty of this sonnet lies in the brilliant risk Keats takes of anticipating his boldest image by launching straight away into metaphors of voyaging. The octave exposes his limited experience of Greek literature with closed rhyme's lulling musicality (sometimes a trap in English): the first quatrain deals with minor writers, 'goodly states' in their way, but surpassed in power by the 'demesne' of Homer which is the subject of the second quatrain. The theme has been fully stated and developed by the time Keats comes to 'turn', so that the sestet demands some bold conviction or surprise. The image of the astronomer acts as a buffer here. The discovery of a new planet is grand but rather vague. It enforces the sense of Keats's receptivity and alertness, but it has little of the power of the final lines. These succeed because 'stout Cortez' is so specific, so far removed from the Mediterranean and so particularly appropriate figuratively to Keats's main point, which is that just as Cortez (though Keats means Balboa) discovers a continent through an ocean (i.e. that he is not in Asia after all) so Keats discovers Homer through Chapman's translation. This is what the 'wild surmise' is all about: the discovery in each case is indirect. Homer and the Pacific remain mysterious, essentially unknown.

It will be clear from this example (an overnight effusion) that the sonnet encourages intelligence, precision and density of imagery. For Keats, indeed, the sonnet was the key to his great Ode stanza. When we consider the substance and the depth of some more modern writers of sonnets (Mallarmé, Rilke, Auden for instance) it will easily be supposed that the sonnet is capable of anything. Without denying the versatility that its continued use in our post-symbolist age has preserved for it, it should be remembered that its prime original use was as a love lyric. The artificiality still associated with the 'Petrarchan' sonnet was introduced by D'Arezzo, who imparted to it those inventions of Provençal love poetry which derived from the *concetti* of the Roman erotic poets and through them of the Greek epigrammatists. Guinizelli, Cavalcanti and Dante, and others of the *dolce stil nuovo*, reacted against this artificiality, and despite the lingering accusations implicit in the term 'Petrarchanism', Petrarch himself insisted on the genuineness of his passion for Laura, the housewife of Avignon whom he met 'in the year 1327, exactly at the hour of prime on the sixth of April', loved for twenty-one years and immortalized in his *Rime*. As love poetry the form was almost irredeemably overworked in the Renaissance, so that Carlyle could remark of Petrarch: 'He might have built a palace and has made some half-a-dozen snuff boxes with invisible lids – very pretty certainly, but useless', and contemporary Victorian critics (even while presiding over the revival of formal Petrarchanism) could turn from the poetry to supposed biographical or confessional elements in the great Elizabethan sonneteers, particularly in Shakespeare who did, after all, build a number of palaces.

By the seventeenth century, however, the possible uses of the sonnet had been extended and codified. Tasso's division of his sonnets into Love Sonnets, Heroical Sonnets and Sacred and Moral Sonnets could be taken to have a wider generic significance for the English tradition – indeed, only the Nature Sonnet, ubiquitous between Bowles and Clare, and not infrequent afterwards, could not with ease be accommodated within it. The clearest example of the shift in emphasis is provided by Milton, whose exercises in the political, biographical and encomiastic were to have great effect upon the Romantics, particularly Wordsworth and Coleridge. We might agree with Landor that Milton 'caught the Sonnet from the dainty hand/Of Love, who cried to lose it; and he gave/The notes to Glory' (*Last Fruit of an Old Tree*, 1853, p. 473), but the essential Miltonic contribution is the importance he gives not to the public element so much as the personal. He described 'How soon hath Time' in a letter to Diodati as 'some of my nightward thoughts ... made up in a Petrarchian stanza, which I told you of', an oddly circumlocutory phrase which none the less describes very well the ultimately autobiographical nature of even his grandest sonnets. The purely occasional may, by contrast, be seen in something like Sylvester's

'Sonnets upon the late Miraculous Peace in France' (*Works*, 1641, pp. 271–8).

Milton is the first great English poet to recognize and cultivate the Italian form. Of his twenty-three sonnets, five have the type 1 sestet, seven type 2 and four type 3. Five of the sonnets were written in Italian. Despite this attention to the legitimate rhyme scheme, Milton has been accused of overriding its formal demands and (by Saintsbury, II, 217) of treating the sonnet as 'not much more than a form of verse-paragraph'. The following example shows why:

> *Cromwell*, our cheif of men, who through a cloud
>   Not of warr only, but detractions rude,
>   Guided by faith and matchless Fortitude
>   To peace and truth thy glorious way has plough'd,
> And on the neck of crowned Fortune proud
>   Hast reard Gods Trophies, and his work pursu'd,
>   While *Darwen* stream with blood of Scotts imbu'd,
>   And *Dunbarr feild* resounds thy praises loud,
> And *Worsters* laureat wreath; yet much remaines
>   To conquer still; peace hath her victories
>   No less renown'd then warr, new foes arise
> Threatning to bind our soules with secular chaines:
>   Helpe us to save free Conscience from the paw
>   Of hireling wolves whose Gospell is their maw.

The sonnet pursues its geographical account of praise of Cromwell well beyond the octave, as though such examples could continue to occur to Milton and indeed demand to be heard. This means that he must turn not before, but *within* line 9 ('yet . . .') and this delay in turn encourages two very strong enjambements in order to accommodate the three statements of the first tercet. The laconic urgency of the passage about the peacetime enemies contrasts magnificently with the steady enumeration of Cromwell's triumphs which has preceded (and, at the delayed turn, compressed) it. It is perhaps a pity, however, that Milton has used here (the only occasion in English that he does so) a form of sestet (cddcee) which yields a final couplet. This has tempted him to a labelling of the Presbyterians which is trivial both in the routine pastoral metaphor and in the satirical chime of the last two lines.

This freedom with the formal structure of the sonnet accords with Milton's own practice elsewhere, but there was already a tendency before him (in Herbert, for instance, or Habington) to enjamb, and to precipitate the sonnet before the turn.

The sonnet in the eighteenth century lives under the shadow of Milton if it can be said to be alive at all. Critics have been tempted by the paucity of its occurrence to search diligently for all possible examples, turning up a couple by Sedley here, one by Stillingfleet there and so on. The most interesting figure is Thomas Edwards who, except for 'An Ode occasioned by a Lady's being burnt with curling irons' wrote only sonnets, fifty of them between 1746 and 1755, all but four in regular Italian form (in 6th edition of his *Canons of Criticism*, 1758). Edwards gave some encouragement to Susannah Highmore, Hester Mulso and William Mason, but it seems nonetheless something of a strain to put back the Petrarchan/Miltonic revival, as Havens does, to the 1730s. The significant moment of revival occurs in the 1780s with the work of Warton, Bowles and Charlotte Smith. A poetry of mood and landscape had use for such an essentially personal form, though Bowles in his Introductory Notice to *Sonnets and other Poems* (1796) was fairly cavalier about its structure. It might as well have fourteen lines as any other number, he said, and the poet could use 'many or few, or no rhymes at all'. Blake's 'To the Evening Star' is unrhymed, but the occurrence is rare. More significantly, the pre-Romantic sonneteers took liberties with the Italian octave, using open rhyme or open mixed with closed rhyme. Warton's 'To the River Lodon' uses abbaabcc:

Ah! what a weary race my feet have run,
Since first I trod thy banks with alders crown'd,
And thought my way was all thro' fairy ground,
Beneath thy azure sky, and golden sun:
Where first my Muse to lisp her notes begun!
While pensive Memory traces back the round,
Which fills the varied interval between;
Much pleasure, more of sorrow, marks the scene.
Sweet native stream! those skies and suns so pure
No more return, to cheer my evening road!
Yet still one joy remains, that not obscure,
Nor useless, all my vacant days have flow'd,
From youth's gay dawn to manhood's prime mature;
Nor with the Muse's laurel unbestow'd.

The turn at least is legitimate, and the sestet formally neat (if smug in sentiment) but something has clearly gone wrong with the octave. The first quatrain has its proper unity, though line 4 lacks incisiveness. Then as if conscious that the quatrain has ended weakly, Warton throws the fifth line after it, failing to give the second quatrain its identity as a developing unit in the poem and rounding off the uncertain syntax of the octave with the misplaced assertiveness of a couplet.

This kind of thing is perhaps indicative of the difficulty inherent in the Italian octave for English poets. Milton got over what Keats called its 'pouncing rhymes' either by heavy enjambement or by a sinewy – even jocular – accentuation of them. Wordsworth, much under the influence of Milton, was keen to emphasize the 'intense unity' of the sonnet, and softened the octave by using abbaacca in nearly half of his over 500 sonnets. But even where Wordsworth is perfectly legitimate, as in the following, eleventh in the River Duddon series (1820), his genius for using the sonnet less as 'a piece of architecture' than as 'an orbicular body, a sphere or a dew-drop' is fully apparent:

No fiction was it of the antique age:
A sky-blue stone, within this sunless cleft,
Is of the very footmarks unbereft
Which tiny Elves impressed; – on that smooth stage
Dancing with all their brilliant equipage
In secret revels – haply after theft
Of some sweet Babe – Flower stolen, and coarse Weed left
For the distracted Mother to assuage
Her grief with, as she might! – But, where, oh! where
Is traceable a vestige of the notes
That ruled those dances wild in character? –
Deep underground? Or in the upper air,
On the shrill wind of midnight? or where floats
O'er twilight fields the autumnal gossamer?

Though Wordsworth still has Warton's interest in fairies, and some of his back-handed diction (compare 'unbereft' and 'un-bestow'd'), this sonnet is a world away from his. At first sight the sonnet's organic life is casual, effusive. But its afterthoughts and parentheses are carefully constructed to conform to his Miltonic interpretation of its basic structure. Its development breaks in just a little earlier than the second quatrain, and allows a brilliantly imaginative and specific motivation for the fairies' revels, including a vignette of the deprived mother – typical Wordsworthian pathos, here given a heartless impulse of excitement as his attention is again diverted to the pagan symbolism of the fairy chasm. He has, of course, overshot the octave and must turn in line 9, at 'But, where, oh! where ...'. This Miltonic licence is well established, however, and allows the controlled rambling of the central lines to distract the reader before he is again firmly set on his course and propelled by the beautifully-paced rhetorical questions of the sestet to the sonnet's conclusion. Ben Jonson had accused the sonnet of his day of being like the bed of Procrustes, 'where some who were too short were racked; and others too long cut short'.

By the time of the Romantics this was just the kind of thing that the sonnet could do deliberately, and with finesse.

The influence of Milton and Wordsworth on the early Victorian sonnet was considerable. It was, in any case, a period when the Italian sonnet was recognized as the legitimate form. Wordsworth can be seen as a model both for descriptive sonneteers such as Charles Tennyson Turner or Frederick Faber, and for ecclesiastical sonneteers like Keble, Newman and Alford: the Oxford Group's *Lyra Apostolica* (1836) devotes 34 of 243 pages to sonnets. Many other Victorian sonneteers (the Rossettis, Patmore and Elizabeth Barrett Browning for example) approximate to Italian models. It is fair to suggest, however, that the Victorian sonnet finds its strength in the sequence. Many individual sonnets fail to achieve the weight and substance that occasional poems really need in order to survive, and relax contentedly (as, for instance, does Tennyson Turner's 'On Finding a Small Fly crushed in a Book') into triviality and piety.

The great exception is Hopkins, who elevated the nineteenth-century religious sonnet into something intellectually and emotionally respectable. He did not feel its intimacy and brevity a disadvantage in dealing with complex subject-matter, and he found it appropriate for all moods, depressed and ecstatic alike. His principal contributions were a restoration of seventeenth-century toughness of language, and the surging expansiveness of sprung rhythm:

> I caught this morning morning's minion, king-
>   dom of daylight's dauphin, dapple-dawn-drawn Falcon in his riding
>   Of the rolling level underneath him steady air, and striding
> High there, how he rung upon the rein of a wimpling wing
> In his ecstasy! then off, off forth on swing,
>   As a skate's heel sweeps smooth on a bow-bend: the hurl and gliding
>   Rebuffed the big wind. My heart in hiding
> Stirred for a bird, – the achieve of, the mastery of the thing!

Brute beauty and valour and act, oh, air, pride, plume, here
    Buckle! AND the fire that breaks from thee then, a billion
Times told lovelier, more dangerous, O my chevalier!

    No wonder of it: shéer plód makes plough down sillion
Shine, and blue-bleak embers, ah my dear,
    Fall, gall themselves, and gash gold-vermilion.

As so often in Hopkins, the metrical spread and energy of the verse render the rhymes slightly absurd, yet the turn is so power-fully employed that it becomes in itself a substitute for a stated argument. The result is a symbolism which has required much puzzled commentary and hazards as to its subject – two aspects of priestly experience, ritual splendour and pastoral drudgery, reflected in the nature of Christ as both hero and sufferer. Pin-pointing the turn is not easy, but the capitalized 'AND' brilliantly conveys the suppressed excitement of Hopkins's main point.

Despite the example of Hopkins, few important modern poets have paid great attention to the legitimate sonnet. In a period of technical innovation such attention has seemed fussy, and minor poets like Lord Alfred Douglas who have persisted with Italian form as 'some deliberate cage/Wherein to keep wild thoughts like birds in thrall' (*Complete Poems*, 1928, p. 77) have been fairly ignored for the quality of those thoughts. There are many excep-tions, of course, and W. H. Auden is one: he writes with freedom and authority, and tends towards the Italian. William Empson (who played a significant part in the revival of early forms like the *villanelle* and the sestina) has two regular Italian sonnets with type 2 sestets ('The Ants' and 'Not wrongly moved . . .'), though a third, 'Rolling the Lawn', has a sestet in couplets, supporting the rather prodding tone of the poem, and a fourth, 'Camping Out', is in the category of curiosity, clogged with rhyme (aabaaab ccdcccd). Empson's freedom is designed, where the freedom of many modern writers of sonnets is merely cavalier, and, in any case, the English sonnet or some hybrid is generally preferred.

2

The English Sonnet

The sonnet made a late appearance in English literature. Chaucer might, of course, have written sonnets if he had wished, but for him the nature of the form went unrecognized. He turned Petrarch's 88th into three stanzas of rhyme royal and used it as Troilus's song in *Troilus and Criseyde* (I. 400–20).

A century and a half later the sonnet found its way to the Tudor court through Wyatt and Surrey. Even then the point of the Italian form was not entirely grasped, for Wyatt's sonnets all ended with a couplet, and Surrey, after some experimentation, used a pattern of alternately rhymed quatrains, which encouraged logical exposition right up to this final couplet and postponed the turn. Thus the English (sometimes 'Shakespearean') sonnet is as follows:

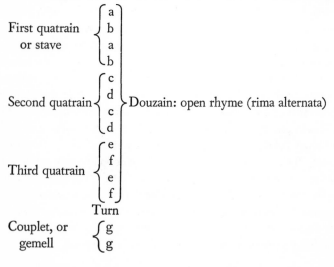

First quatrain or stave
$\begin{cases} a \\ b \\ a \\ b \end{cases}$

Second quatrain
$\begin{cases} c \\ d \\ c \\ d \end{cases}$ } Douzain: open rhyme (rima alternata)

Third quatrain
$\begin{cases} e \\ f \\ e \\ f \end{cases}$

Turn

Couplet, or gemell
$\begin{cases} g \\ g \end{cases}$

The early discovery of the characteristic couplet of the English sonnet is shrouded in mystery. Saintsbury (I, 308) was tempted to see its origin in Wyatt's use of two stanzas of rhyme royal ('was never file yet half so well yfilèd'), but this has been dismissed by Bullock who points out that Wyatt would have found sonnets with cdd/cdd sestets that could be read cddc/dd (e.g. by Cino da Pistoia in *Raccolta dei Giunti*, 1527). No doubt the reliance on the couplet is of a piece with Wyatt's metrical irregularity. This has been said to be deliberate, or to be derived from the 'pausing line' of medieval verse, but the older view, that Wyatt was an uncertain experimentalist, is probably right after all.

The English form, whatever the role of accident or error in its invention, certainly became popular. As Prince points out, only two sonnets in *Tottel's Miscellany* (1557) after Wyatt and Surrey recur to Italian form, and it became the staple pattern of the Elizabethan sequence, enshrined in such theoretical pronouncements as this of Gascoigne's: 'Then have you Sonnets, some thinke that all Poemes (being short) may be called Sonnets, as in deede it is a diminutive worde derived of *sonare*, but yet I can beste allowe to call those Sonnets which are of fourtene lynes, every line conteyning tenne syllables. The firste twelve do ryme in staves of four lines by crosse meetre, and the last twoo ryming togither do conclude the whole' (*Works*, Cambridge, 1907, I, 471 f.). There is no doubt that English poets, finding their language harder to rhyme in than Italian poets, clung to a sonnet in seven rhymes as something of itself more congenial than a sonnet in four or five rhymes.

But the greater flexibility in rhyming is not the main difference between English and Italian form. More important is the difference of effect in the proportions eight to six and twelve to two, particularly in the ending of the sonnet, where the couplet makes the English sonnet seem particularly summary or epigrammatic. The following example is by Surrey:

Norfolk sprang thee, Lambeth holds thee dead,
Clere of the County of Cleremont, though hight;
Within the wombe of Ormondes race thou bread,
And sawest thy cosine crowned in thy sight.
Shelton for love, Surrey for Lord thou chase:
Ay me, while life did last that league was tender;
Tracing whose steps thou sawest Kelsall blaze,
Laundersey burnt, and battered Bullen render.
At Muttrell gates, hopeles of all recure,
Thine Earle, halfe dead, gave in thy hand his Will;
Which cause did thee this pining death procure,
Ere Sommers four times seaven thou couldest fulfill.
    Ah Clere, if love had booted, care, or cost,
    Heaven had not wonn, nor Earth so timely lost.

As a confessed epitaph, the sonnet makes good use of the last-minute turn. Clere's good connexions (related to Anne Boleyn) are presented in the first quatrain. His purely voluntary relationships ('chase' = 'chose') follow, in the second quatrain; and, arising from his association with Surrey, his selfless attention to the wounded Earl at the siege of Montreuil, leading to his death, occupies the third quatrain. There is logical development here: by contrast between the first and second quatrains and by example between the second and third. The points thus made are that whatever the status of one's birth one does not choose it, and that love and friendship are on the other hand a matter of choice, though not of calculation. The sonnet does not avoid suggesting that Clere's background in fact provides just that kind of nobility which line 13 perhaps praises for being reckless, but the tone of the turn ('Ah, Clere!') sufficiently raises an ambiguity in the paradox by offering the love as not Clere's, but Surrey's.

Just as it is hard in the Italian sonnet to use the second quatrain for constructive organic development, the three isolated quatrains of the English sonnet are similarly prone to simple variation or repetition. Ideally there should be even greater tension in the proposition of the English sonnet, three turns of the screw so to speak, before the point is driven home in the couplet. In practice this is not often so, and Prince has gone so far as to characterize the form as sharply as this: 'The movement away from Italian form is a sign of life, but for the most part of a bubbling or frothing kind of life, which develops melody, prettiness, smoothness, gaiety, or mere silly fancy at the expense of all else'. For Fussell (p. 128) the English douzain and couplet 'invites images of balloons and pins'.

It may be agreed that turning at line 9 and resolving in six lines is a steadier and subtler process than turning at line 13 and resolving in two, though the couplet clearly answers an English need for encapsulation (whether lyrical, gnomic or witty) and one must not forget that the legitimate form of the sonnet has a tendency to assert itself in the shape of a frequent minor turn at the third quatrain. The following is by Drayton:

> Since ther's no helpe, Come let us kisse and part,
> Nay, I have done: You get no more of Me,
> And I am glad, yea glad with all my heart
> That thus so cleanly, I my Selfe can free,
> Shake hands for ever, Cancell all our Vowes,
> And when We meet at any time againe,
> Be it not seene in either of our Browes,
> That We one jot of former Love Reteyne;
> Now at the last gaspe, of Loves latest Breath,
> When his Pulse fayling, Passion speechlesse lies,
> When Faith is kneeling by his bed of Death,
> And Innocence is closing up his Eyes,
>   Now if thou woulds't, when all have given him over,
>   From Death to Life, thou might'st him yet recover.
>   (*Ideas Mirrour* 61)

The 'Now' of line 9 is merely a forecast of the 'Now' of line 13, a preparatory metaphorical elaboration of the couplet's very English *volte face*, and yet it acts as a preparatory turn in itself, particularly as the first two quatrains (not in substance organically developed) are grammatically so closely linked. The feminine rhymes in the 'gemell' accentuate its comic careless conviction. It is perhaps worth mentioning that sonnets in Italian invariably use feminine rhyme, achieving a musical effect impossible in English. For whereas in English feminine rhymes tend towards lightness of tone, in Italian it is masculine rhymes which do so (and sonnets using masculine rhymes are called 'mute' sonnets). An English sonnet which uses only feminine rhymes, incidentally (like Shakespeare 20), can sound very bland.

Sidney, who uses the Italian octave and very commonly a cdcdee sestet, can preserve the two tercets of Italian form through syntax (cdc/dee) while acknowledging the pressure of English form through the rhymes (cdcd/ee). This he probably learned from Wyatt, and it enables him to achieve a striking complexity of form:

> Having this day my horse, my hand, my launce
> >   Guided so well, that I obtain'd the prize,
> >   Both by the judgment of the English eyes,
> And of some sent from that sweet enemie *Fraunce*;
> Horsemen my skill in horsemanship advaunce;
> >   Towne-folkes my strength; a daintier judge applies
> >   His praise to sleight, which from good use doth rise;
> Some luckie wits impute it but to chaunce;
> >   Others because of both sides I do take
> My bloud from them who did excell in this,
> >   Thinke Nature me a man of armes did make.
> How farre they shot awrie! the true cause is,
> >   *Stella* lookt on, and from her heavenly face
> >   Sent forth the beames, which made so faire my race.
>
> *(Astrophil and Stella* 41)

If we read this with Italian structure in mind we find a contrast, in octave and sestet, between Sidney's equestrian abilities and his true motivation, between the superficial exercise of skill, strength or sleight and even luck, and the real cause of his success. We sense an opposition between accidental acquired qualities (octave) and essential given qualities (sestet), enabling us to read the tercets as thus linked even in their distinction between heredity and astrology. The Italian octave fully supports this, and the sestet is indeed syntactically organized into tercets.

But if we read the sonnet with the English structure in mind, we can see a rather different organization – a douzain (in which the first quatrain states Sidney's success, the second the views of those who attribute it to nurture and the third the views of those who attribute it to nature) and a couplet which solves the problem. One's sense that the English structure predominates is reinforced by a couplet introducing Stella (as in other sonnets) as a kind of *dea ex machina*, and by the neatness with which the misguided judges are eclipsed by Stella in the role not only of beneficent star, but of judge herself.

Such a reversal is supported by the very terms of Sidney's sequence (the 'star-lover' and the 'star'). In cases where the couplet's conclusion is not so prepared for, its brevity can more easily call forth accusations of wit and paradox in the English turn, since there is not the space of the Italian sestet to make an argued resolution. The couplet must assert. An example from Shakespeare (Sonnet 65) shows how it may be used to counter an overwhelming case assembled by the preceding quatrains:

> Since brasse, nor stone, nor earth, nor boundlesse sea,
> But sad mortallity ore-swaies their power,
> How with this rage shall beautie hold a plea,
> Whose action is no stronger then a flower?
> O how shall summers hunny breath hold out
> Against the wrackfull siedge of battring dayes,
> When rocks impregnable are not so stoute,
> Nor gates of steele so strong but time decayes?

> O fearfull meditation, where alack,
> Shall times best Jewell from times chest lie hid?
> Or what strong hand can hold his swift foote back,
> Or who his spoile of beautie can forbid?
>> O none, unlesse this miracle have might,
>> That in black inck my love may still shine bright.

Only the aside 'O fearfull meditation' at line 9, by providing a moment of conscious distancing from Shakespeare's appalled account of the world's ephemerality, pays any sort of regard to the Italian turn. Since an apostrophe occurs also at lines 5 and 13, pointing the division into quatrains and couplet, the sonnet's effect is (until the real turn) cumulative in the English manner. In the first quatrain the pattern is established: beauty pleads in vain with mortality. In the ensuing quatrains the point is emphasized by the urgency of the rhetoric, and by the development of the symbols for love's precarious object ('beautie' ... 'summers hunny breath' ... 'time's best Jewell'). It is the very lack of qualifying development up to line 12 that makes up so strong a case for mortality against the futile hopes of the lover, and so presents the consolation of poetry's 'immortality' in the couplet as a kind of half-serious Quixotic gesture. The feeling is that something so witty ('black inck ... shine bright') might be true since it is on such a different conceptual plane from the magnificent gloom of the douzain, and that only something as perfunctorily expressed as this *could* begin to be miraculous. Shakespeare uses the sonnet's final couplet in many different ways, of course, but the effect here could in fairness be said to be typical of the English sonnet at its height.

One important variety of the English sonnet was invented by Spenser. He had, at the age of 17, put some of Du Bellay's *Songe* into unrhymed quatorzains (*A Theatre for Worldlings*, 1569). Despite the lack of rhyme these approximated in cadence and syntax to sonnet form, and are interesting to compare with their rhymed counterparts in his *Visions of Bellay* (1591). Spenser was not satisfied with the tendency towards discreteness in Surrey's English form, however, and used in his *Amoretti* (1595) an English form with linked rhyme analogous to his *Faerie Queene* stanza. Such a pattern reintroduces the couplets characteristic of the Italian sonnet, and, by blending the quatrains together, offers the opportunity for more closely developed argument:

First quatrain
{
a
b
a
b } couplet link

Second quatrain
{
b
c
b
c } couplet link

Third quatrain
{
c
d
c
d

Couplet
{
e
e

The following example (*Amoretti* 75) shows how the increased musicality of the Spenserian form could compensate for the weakness of argument to which Spenser himself as a poet was sometimes prone:

> One day I wrote her name upon the strand,
>   but came the waves and washed it away:
>   agayne I wrote it with a second hand,
>   but came the tyde, and made my paynes his pray.
> Vayne man, sayd she, that doest in vaine assay,
>   a mortall thing so to immortalize,
>   for I my selve shall lyke to this decay,

and eek my name bee wyped out lykewize.
Not so, (quod I) let baser things devize
to dy in dust, but you shall live by fame:
my verse your vertues rare shall eternize,
and in the heavens wryte your glorious name.
Where whenas death shall all the world subdew,
our love shall live, and later life renew.

The quatrains define the situation and the ensuing dialogue as in many an ordinary English sonnet, but Spenser's couplet links and the bountiful alliteration which accompanies them turn the whole thing into a melodious game. Moreover, a certain lulling structural underpattern is set up in the arrangement of the lines by distichs – an arrangement made possible largely through the fullness of rhyme of the Spenserian form. The result is a very different kind of assertiveness from Shakespeare's on the same theme, an assertiveness not confined to the couplet, and not therefore dignified with wit. The essential similarity of paper to sand remains, despite the introduction of 'the heavens' (more conventional than Shakespeare's 'miracle' of art), so that we maintain a critical distance from the aspirations of the poet. Though perhaps the point is (as with all poems on the theme) that as long as the sonnet survives to be read its assertion will be true. This is not a fact that the poet should too carelessly rely on.

The Elizabethans used the English sonnet to exhaustion. Its late history is, on the whole, one of assimilation (in conditions of experiment or licence) with the Italian sonnet. Herbert, in his few sonnets, seemed to prefer closed rhyme in the third quatrain, allowing either two tercets or quatrain and couplet (eff/egg; effe/gg) with greater aplomb even than the Sidneyan sestet. Donne, like Milton, presided over the general blurring of the sonnet's musical form. Here, for instance, we see an Italian octave followed by an enclosed quatrain and couplet:

Death, be not proud, though some have called thee
Mighty and dreadfull, for, thou art not soe,
For, those, whom thou think'st, thou dost overthrow,
Die not, poor death, nor yet canst thou kill mee.
From rest and sleepe, which but thy pictures bee,
Much pleasure, then from thee, much more must flow,
And soonest our best men with thee doe go,
Rest of their bones, and soules deliverie.
Thou art slave to Fate, Chance, kings, and desperate men,
And dost with poison, warre and sicknesse dwell,
And poppie, or charmes can make us sleepe as well,
And better than thy stroake; why swell'st thou then?
One short sleepe past, wee wake eternally,
And death shall be no more; death, thou shalt die.

It will be observed that the rhyme scheme is identical with Milton's
sonnet on Cromwell which I included in the previous chapter as an
example of Italian form. But attention to the structure of these two
poems will reveal their divergence. Donne feels no obligation to
turn at line 9 or anywhere near it, whereas he clearly feels the
quatrains as developing units: (1) Death's power a pretence; (2)
Death as a welcome release; (3) Death's essential weakness. These
aspects of death are linked in service of the apocalyptic solution in
the couplet, already foreshadowed in the first quatrain, and careful
enjambement within (but not across) the quatrains emphasizes
their individuality. For this reason it is difficult to read the last six
lines as two tercets: the enjambement at line 11 is too strong, and
the words 'why swell'st thou then' look rather backwards than for-
wards. But the couplet itself is not a unity in the conventional way,
even though it is witty, for the wit is delayed till the final phrase:
indeed, the effect is of a turn four *words* from the end of the sonnet.

Between Milton and Wordsworth the English form is not much
in evidence, though the process of assimilation makes its characteristics familiar even in sonnets ostensibly modelled on the Italian,
e.g. Gray's 'On the Death of Mr Richard West' (ababababcdcdcd)

with its powerfully elegaic open rhyme, or Cowper's 'To Mrs Unwin' (abbaabbacdcdee) beautifully turned at both sestet and couplet.

An interesting example of sonneteering practice is provided by Coleridge's 'Sonnets on Eminent Characters' (1794–5). Of the twelve in the series, eight are in English form (though closed rhyme predominates in the first two quatrains); one is Italian form (type 2 sestet); one adds a type 5 sestet to two closed-rhyme quatrains; and two are very mixed form (ababbcbcdedfef; ababcddceffefe). Since Coleridge referred to his 'series of *Sonnets* (as it is the fashion to call them)' we might expect a cavalier treatment of the form. In fact Coleridge had already experimented, in about 1793, as Keats and Shelley were to experiment, with a more organic form in 'To the River Otter' (ababbcdcdcdece) and his political sonnets represent a polite gesture towards English form (even the Italian sonnet is printed as three quatrains and a couplet) which frequently runs at odds with their powerful Miltonic flavour. Clearly for some writers variety of rhyme and a concluding couplet could still play their part in the organic Romantic sonnet:

> O what a loud and fearful shriek was there,
>   As though a thousand souls one death-groan pour'd!
>   Ah me! thy saw beneath a Hireling's sword
> Their Koskiusko fall! through the swart air
> (As pauses the tir'd Cossac's barbarous yell
>   Of Triumph) on the chill and midnight gale
>   Rises with frantic burst or sadder swell
> The dirge of murder'd Hope! while Freedom pale
> Bends in such anguish o'er her destin'd bier,
>   As if from eldest time some Spirit meek
>   Had gather'd in a mystic urn each tear
> That ever on a Patriot's furrow'd cheek
> Fit channel found; and she had drain'd the bowl
> In the mere wilfulness, and sick despair of soul.
>
> (No. V: Koskiusko)

None of the constituent parts of this sonnet coincides exactly with the conventional divisions of its English form, and yet it is clear that there are four aspects of the subject which bear some relation to the form's four elements. The vision of the failure of Koskiusko's revolt falls short of a first quatrain. The symbolized outcry is elaborated in a passage which, again, falls short of the second quatrain but which is equal in length, including the half-lines, to a quatrain. The consequent notion of the death of Freedom overruns the third quatrain, and by a similar computation totals five lines – for the insistently climactic rhyming of the couplet is deliberately divorced syntactically from what precedes it, and in its sibilant and labial brevity provides a suitably whispered yet sonorous cadence to the close. The sonnet, through its liberated straddling of prosodic convention (perhaps expressible as $3\frac{1}{2} + \frac{1}{2}3\frac{1}{2} + \frac{1}{2}4\frac{1}{2} + \frac{1}{2}1$), is enabled to mimic a crescendo of gloomy feeling that runs counter to a diminuendo in actual sound described in the poem. This is the sort of instinctive sleight-of-hand that the true sonneteer can muster. There is much to criticize in this youthful poem, but its rhetoric and inconsistencies (why should a Patriot's tears be poisonous?) are wholly forgotten in the splendid movement of the sonnet, its quite individual musical shape.

There was, from this point, no great sense of tradition in the English sonnet. The Italian again became the legitimate, and though sonnets on the Surrey/Shakespeare model continued to be written (Coleridge himself returned in 'To Asra' and 'Farewell to Love' to the strict form) there is no real evidence of constructive development. One might except the bastard form of Cowper's sonnet mentioned above (abbaabbacdcdee) which became very popular: evidently there was some pressure at the Petrarchan revival to adopt closed rhyme, though many poets, for reasons that we have seen, were unwilling to forego the couplet. In recent times the attraction of the Italian form has been manifest even in sonnets of great freedom, carelessness or experiment, but the couplet is now very strongly associated with the form. It is generally recognized that though the choices that were open to the Romantic poets remain, further technical advances in the form have been and will be essentially minor. Some of these structural and metrical possibilities are discussed in the following chapter.

3
Variants and Curosities

For some time in the sixteenth century poets were not entirely clear (or pretended not to be entirely clear) what exactly a sonnet was. The derivation of the word (from 'sonare') allowed it to be applied carelessly to any sort of lyric or ballad. Donne's *Songs and Sonets* (a title no doubt influenced by Tottel's famous miscellany) contains no sonnets, and Henry King and Kynaston still used the term to mean a love-lyric. In the eighteenth century Collins and Goldsmith used it to mean a short song.

Such misuse is not particularly important, though work in the spirit of the sonnet which is not actually in sonnet form is fairly common in the sixteenth century. Tofte's *Laura* (1597) is a sequence of mostly twelve-line poems, and Barnes's *Parthenophil and Parthenope* (1593) contains many quinzains. An early Elizabethan sequence, Watson's 'Ἑκατομπαθία (1582), uses 'sonnets' of eighteen lines (in three sestets) though Watson succumbed to the quatorzain in his *Tears of Fancy* (1593). The legitimacy of this kind of thing is really only acceptable in a sequence, where the intention and effect of the whole override to a certain extent the grave departure of its parts from the legitimate form whose definition and practice I have already shown to be strict and firmly established. The problem has re-emerged more recently in cases like Meredith's 'Modern Love' (1862), a sequence of sixteen-line poems, or Wallace Stevens's 'Le Monocle de mon Oncle' (*Harmonium*, 1923), a sequence of eleven-line unrhymed poems, both of which in very different ways have the characteristic feel of sonnet sequences even though they cannot be said to be made up

c

of sonnets. Meredith's form has been used by Roy Fuller in 'Meredithian Sonnets' (*Collected Poems*, 1969, pp. 238–48).

On the other hand, sonnets can turn up where least expected. I'm not thinking so much of the hidden 'sonnet' in Milton's *Paradise Lost* referred to by Wordsworth (see Crabb Robinson's *Diary*, 1869, III, 86), or the frequent fourteen-line paragraphs in Pope's *Essay on Man* (such as 'Lo! The poor Indian') for these merely by coincidence support the quatorzain as a common and useful compass for ratiocination. The dialogue sonnet in *Romeo and Juliet* (I. v. 95 ff.) is a real sonnet, but also an interesting extension of its function, acutely described by Fussell (p. 128): 'The two lovers find in the structure of the English sonnet the perfect vehicle for what is less an emotional experience than a mock-academic *débat*'. Another example of the submerged sonnet might be Eliot's 'The time is now propitious, as he guesses' (*The Waste Land*, ll. 235–48) which is in regular English form except for the assonance of the couplet ('kiss'/'unlit'). Though the manuscripts reveal this to be quite fortuitous it is fair to say that the encounter of the secretary and the estate agent's clerk gains something from this ironical allusion to sonnet-form and therefore to an ideal love.

Variations of the form come into existence through a desire to explore legitimate possibilities and to provide genuine extensions of its capabilities. Thus we find that, except for instances where words themselves are abandoned (see the picture-riddle sonnet described by Mönch, p. 45 f.), variants do comment constructively on the sonnet-form and of course frequently become successful poems in their own right.

Of structural variants, the most radical have been condensed and expanded sonnets. Recognizing the structural cadence inherent in the Italian sonnet, Hopkins attempted to preserve the proportions and effect of octave and sestet in a shorter poem. He called

'Peace' and 'Pied Beauty' curtal (i.e. curtailed) sonnets, using the rhyme scheme abcabc/$\left\{\begin{array}{l} \text{dcbdc} \\ \text{dbcdc} \end{array}\right.$ in the proportion $6:4\frac{1}{2}$.

When will you ever, Peace, wild wooddove, shy wings shut,
Your round me roaming end, and under be my boughs?
When, when, Peace, will you, Peace? I'll not play hypocrite

To own my heart: I yield you do come sometimes; but
That piecemeal peace is poor peace. What pure peace allows
Alarm of wars, the daunting wars, the death of it?

O surely, reaving Peace, my Lord should leave in lieu
Some good! And so he does leave Patience exquisite,
That plumes to Peace thereafter. And when Peace here does house
He comes with work to do, he does not come to coo,
    He comes to brood and sit.

                                            ('Peace')

It is not clear if the characteristic effect of the sonnet is entirely preserved here, for (despite the alexandrines) the brevity accentuates the slight lyrical quality of the thought.

The expanded sonnet can more easily retain the functional parts of its original. The third sonnet of Auden's 'The Quest' is of this kind, using the rhyme scheme aabcbcddecec/fghifgigh in the proportion 12:9. Auden's rhyming cunningly offsets the potential bulkiness of the form, for the 'octave' is constructed of two sestets of the fifth type and is both musically effective and reminiscent of familiar sonnet rhyming, while the 'sestet' is of an original arrangement whereby weak h rhymes ('impossible'/'all') and enjambement at line 19 allow the strong g rhymes ('say'/'betray'/'day') and f rhymes ('fear'/'year' with a firmly end-stopped line 17) to do all the work. Variations of this kind seem to work best in sequences where they can be made to express some point, or break up the progression of regular sonnets.

Inversion of octave and sestet has been tried. Rupert Brooke's

'Sonnet Reversed' (1911) is the best example, indeed a successful *tour-de-force* in its own right. Sassoon has several quatorzains beginning with couplet or sestet, but only Brooke uses the inverted form as an essential element in the meaning of the poem (which is appropriately directed against the idealistic treatment of love embodied in the Petrarchan tradition). The couplet dramatizes the bliss of a honeymoon after which life never again captures such intensity, and the sonnet works its way through to an octave expository of the long anti-climax of a petit-bourgeois existence:

> Hand trembling towards hand; the amazing lights
> Of heart and eye. They stood on supreme heights.
>
> Ah, the delirious weeks of honeymoon!
>   Soon they returned, and, after strange adventures,
> Settled at Balham by the end of June.
>   Their money was in Can. Pacs. B. Debentures,
> And in Antofagastas. Still he went
>   Cityward daily; still she did abide
> At home. And both were really quite content
>   With work and social pleasures. Then they died.
> They left three children (besides George, who drank):
>   The eldest Jane, who married Mr Bell,
> William, the head-clerk in the County Bank,
>   And Henry, a stock-broker, doing well.

Brooke's satire may seem dated, but such a brilliant technical *trouvaille* keeps the poem very fresh. Most of the ten sonnets of Dylan Thomas's 'Altarwise by Owl-light' sequence (1936) put a type 3 sestet in front of an English octave, though Thomas has on the whole abandoned rhyme for assonance. It is not easy to see the purpose of this inversion, however, since progression of thought or feeling in the sonnets is elusive, and in only a few cases is there anything like a turn at line 7.

In the fourteenth century there was a vogue for the satirical *sonetto caudato* (tailed sonnet) in which a couplet was added after the second tercet. Milton's 'On the New Forcers of Conscience under the Long Parliament' adds six lines (two couplets each preceded by a half-line which rhymes with the line it follows) to allow him through insistence and perseverance to raise his scornful voice even more loudly against the Presbyterians than he could manage in a conventional fourteen lines. This kind of coda was imitated by Hopkins in 'Tom's Garland'. Hopkins wrote: 'I wanted the coda for a sonnet which is in some sort "nello stilo satirico o bernesco". It has a kind of rollic at all events. The coda is an immense resource to have.' Hopkins used five more or less regularly-placed 'burden-lines' to extend 'Harry Ploughman' in a rather different way: the lines are choric, stressing and echoing the material they follow in the body of the sonnet. His 'That Nature is a Heraclitean Fire and of the comfort of the Resurrection' uses three codas and an extra burden-line at the end. This 'sonnet' is a monster, though Hopkins knew very well what he was doing.

Varieties of rhyme-scheme within the conventional structure of the Italian or English sonnet, though not limitless, are nonetheless too great to be adequately dealt with here. Most varieties are nonce-usages justified (or not, as the case may be) by the particular use to which they are put. A good number may be found in the work of Merrill Moore who wrote 'something in excess of fifty-thousand' (see Radcliffe Squires, *Allen Tate: A Literary Biography*, New York, 1971). A division into two equal parts may be observed in Wyatt's 'was never file yet half so well yfilèd', which appears to be made up of two stanzas in rhyme royal (see p. 15), but equal division is not often attempted by poets who have understood the point of the sonnet. English sonnets with closed rhyme in the quatrains are common enough (particularly in America), and such schemes as George Barker's abcdabcdefgefg ('To my Mother', *Eros in Dogma*, 1944, p. 55) will be found to work well enough to have been imitated (and anticipated). The kind of inimitable and unpredictable scheme I originally had in mind is fairly represented by Bandello's abbacdedcddffa (see *Nuova Antologia*, CXXIX, 1907, p. 730).

More irregular rhyme-schemes are only relevant where they have some meaning or point. Unrhymed quatorzains like Spenser's (see p. 20) or Blake's (see p. 9), though due no doubt to ignorance or sublime indifference, do, through organization and syntax, have much of the feel of sonnets, and the same could be said of such modern examples as Herbert Read's 'A Northern Legion' (*Collected Poems*, 1966, p. 146) or W. H. Auden's 'The Secret Agent' (*Collected Shorter Poems*, 1966, p. 22). More formality is provided by the *jeux d'esprit* christened the 'unrhymable sonnet' based on the curious fact that Swann and Sidgwick in their *The Making of Verse* (London, 1937, p. 47) list just fourteen words for which there are no rhymes in English (see the *New Statesman*, vol. 72, 12 August 1966, p. 239). The most interesting example, though, is Robert Lowell's *Notebook* (rev. 1970) consisting of over 360 largely unrhymed quatorzains. Lowell expressly wishes to avoid 'the themes and gigantism of the sonnet', though one wonders why he should have been drawn so far and no further in his formal choice for a set of finely-wrought poems (like Milton's) on public and private themes. Lowell occasionally rounds off twelve lines of blank verse with a couplet, an effective reminder of the English sonnet's wraith haunting the sequence. This, of course, is not new (see, for instance, Christopher Caudwell's 'Twenty Sonnets of Wm Smith', *Poems*, 1965, pp. 23–36, nos. 4, 5, 6, 8, 9, 10, 12, 14, 15, 16, 17 and 19).

Sonnets in two rhymes are capable of a powerful formal duality suitable to certain themes. Examples are Mallarmé's 'Sonnet allegorique de lui-même' ('-ix' and 'or') and *Astrophil and Stella* 89 ('night' and 'day'). The former seems almost deliberately to be a symbolist exercise in the manner of currently popular *bouts-rimés* ('le sens . . . est évoqué par un mirage interne des mots même' said Mallarmé). In the latter case we have an example of the iterating sonnet, where actual rhyme words are repeated. This is quite an early sonnet-variant and may be found in Folgore da San Gemignano's 'Fior de Virtú si e Zentil Corazo' or in Petrarch 16. An interesting example is Leigh Hunt's 'Iterating Sonnet' (*Poetical Works*, 1923, p. 253) where every line ends with the phrase 'United States'. This would, I suppose, be a case of a sonnet in one rhyme, and is not a joke that could stand much repetition.

'Sonnets' of seven couplets are frequent (Herrick wrote one, for instance, there are two by Philip Ayres, and there are fourteen specimens in Arthur Symons's *Amoris Victima*) but if this variant is permissible we would have to begin to consider such things as Pope's 'Lo! the poor Indian' (see p. 28) more seriously. It does, however, provide variety within a sequence, as in Shakespeare 126 or Auden 'The Quest' 14 and 'Petition'.

Shelley and Keats worked hard to discover a more complex and tightly knit arrangement of rhymes, Shelley's 'Ozymandias' with ababacdcedefef and Keats's 'If by dull rhymes' with abcabdcabcdede, but these arrangements, like those of Coleridge in 'To the River Otter' and some of John Clare's, lack the sonnet's musical shape and are not compulsively imitable. Keats's ode stanza (ababcdecde) was one result of his desire to 'discover a better sonnet stanza than we have'. According to Keats 'the legitimate does not suit the language over-well from the pouncing rhymes – the other kind appears too elegaic – and the couplet at the end of it has seldom a pleasing effect'. The ode stanza thus combines an English quatrain and an Italian sestet to avoid these 'pouncing rhymes', 'elegaic' open rhyming, and concluding couplet tags. Shelley produced a novel variety in 'Ode to the West Wind' which should be printed (though it is not always so) as a sequence of five 'sonnets' to the scheme ababcbcdcdedee, whose reliance on Italian *terza rima* seems appropriate and decorous.

Of metrical variants there is not a great deal to be said. Purists will demand the iambic pentameter as the basic metrical unit and

indeed it is the norm – though as may be expected almost every-
thing else has been tried, from the sprung alexandrines of Hopkins's
'That Nature is a Heraclitean Fire' down to the monosyllables
of Jules de Rességuier (whom it is hardly wasteful to quote in
full: 'Fort/Belle,/Elle/Dort;/Sort/Frêle,/Quelle/Mort!/Rose/Close,/
La/Brise/L'a/Prise'). Lines of foot-length may be found in Ashby
-Sterry's anapaestic 'A Shorthand Sonnet written on the fan
of a flirt' (*The Lazy Ministrel*, 1886) which is hardly more sub-
stantial than the foregoing, and lines of two feet in P. Jacopo
Bassani's 'Gentil Vinegia' (1727). Tetrameters are quite common
(e.g. Shakespeare 145, Auden 'The Quest' 19) and in these cases
provide a refreshing change of pace in a sequence. However, as
Saintsbury remarked (II, 150): 'As the Alexandrine is too heavy,
so the octosyllable is too light for the sonnet' and one would not
wish their use to become a habit. *Astrophil and Stella* I is entirely
in alexandrines, while Lofft (p. xxii) has an example in alternate
long and short lines. This kind of metrical variation *within* a
sonnet can be very attractive. It was fairly common in the eighteenth century, for instance, for an alexandrine to be used in the
last line, perhaps by analogy with the Spenserian stanza which was
enjoying a revival (see the Coleridge example on p. 24). Edna St
Vincent Millay uses a final line of seven feet in her seventeen
'Sonnets from an Ungrafted Tree' (*Collected Sonnets*, 1941).
Abbreviated endings were introduced more recently through the
practice of Rilke in *Sonnette an Orpheus*, where they cropped up as
one aspect of his use of a strongly dactylic short metre, as in the
conclusion of number 11 in part 2:

> Toten ist eine Gestalt unseres wandernden Trauerns ...
> Rein ist im heiteren Geist,
> was an uns selber geschicht.
> (Killing is one form of our restless Grief.
> It is pure, to the calmer spirit,
> What happens to us ourselves.)

This kind of laconic yet elegaic ending has been successfully used by Auden in his 'Sonnets from China' 12:

> Here war is harmless like a monument:
> A telephone is talking to a man;
> Flags on a map declare that troops were sent;
> A boy brings milk in bowls. There is a plan
>
> For living men in terror of their lives,
> Who thirst at nine who were to thirst at noon,
> Who can be lost and are, who miss their wives
> And, unlike an idea, can die too soon.
>
> Yet ideas can be true, although men die:
> For we have seen a myriad faces
> Ecstatic from one lie,
>
> And maps can really point to places
> Where life is evil now.
> Nanking. Dachau.

In this contrast of appearance and reality, of theory and praxis, Auden puts great weight upon the place where these collide, where the map becomes life: in the near-spondees of the last line. The effect is at once choked and funereal. 'War' is abstract, and an idea or a plan remote from human misery, and yet in these places, in the midst of the Sino-Japanese war and Nazi Germany in 1938, the embodiment of evil is absolute. The sonnet, by avoiding the full musical statement, implies that there is nothing more to say. The silence is pregnant. Yet the short line itself acts musically, tolling like a bell.

This range of metrical effects is about all that is important for the sonnet. A sonnet could be written in Latin hexameters (there is one by Stephanus Aelius of 1535) but that kind of rhythm is crippling. The flexibilities of the iambic pentameter tradition are more than adequate, given the sonnet's prosodic structure. Nor is there very much left to do with this structure that has permanent significance for the form. It is possible, it seems, for John Updike to write a 'Love Sonnet' almost without words (*Midpoint and Other Poems*, 1969, p. 66), but its point lies as much with its weary but good-humoured recognition of the English sonnet's conventional punctuation as with its flip sexual onomatopoeia:

In Love's rubber armor I come to you,

                                        b
                oo
                                    b.
            c,
                    d
                    c
                    d:
            e
        f———
            e
            f.
                    g
                    g.

Most of the real departures from the form as I have so far described it turn out to be impatient short cuts, simple misunderstandings, or overambitious extensions (see p. 48 for some varieties invented by Roubaud). It remains to discuss an important technical function of the sonnet, that is as a unit within a larger whole: the sonnet-sequence.

4
Sequences

I have said little about the function of the sonnet, because even its slight form is capable of too much to be discussed adequately here. Its range is indeed very wide: from satire like that of Brooke (see p. 30) or Hood's more wistful and brilliant 'Sonnet to Vauxhall', through Shakespeare's wit and invective or Leigh Hunt's grotesqueries to Milton's sublime scorn; from the wary tenderness of Wyatt to the intelligence and passion of Elizabeth Barrett Browning; from Auden's potted literary biographies to Wordsworth's ecclesiastical history. Minutiae in Clare, generalities in Hartley Coleridge, symbolism in Yeats; devotion and piety, doubt and effusion; political tributes, dedications, diary entries: the uses of the sonnet are not easily limitable.

One aspect of its use, however, is too central to be ignored and raises a number of technical questions. This is the popularity of the cycle or sequence of sonnets. Though the poise of the successful single sonnet ensures it a place among the most finished of forms, most poets who have been attracted to it have not been content until they have used the sonnet as an element in a larger whole, providing a succession of variations on a given theme or situation. Such a temptation, without organizing control and perspective, can have its dangers, as the surfeit of sonneteering in, for instance, the late sixteenth century shows.

But there is obviously some inherent urge in the Elizabethan period to celebrate the vagaries of love, not merely in the Petrarchan mode, but to a Petrarchan extent, as the following list of principal sonneteers makes clear:

1582   Watson: Ἑκατομπαθία
1584   Soowthern: *Pandora*
1591   Sidney: *Astrophil and Stella*
1592   Daniel: *Delia*
1593   Watson: *The Tears of Fancie*
1593   Barnes: *Parthenophil and Parthenope*
1593   Lodge: *Phillis*
1593   Fletcher: *Licia*
1594   Constable: *Diana*
1594   *Anon*: *Zepheria*
1594   Percy: *Coelia*
1594   Drayton: *Ideas Mirrour*
1595   Spenser: *Amoretti*
1595   Barnfield: *Cynthia*
1595   E.C.: *Emaricdulfe*
1596   Griffin: *Fidessa*
1596   Linche: *Diella*
1596   Smith: *Chloris*
1597   Tofte: *Laura*
1604   Alexander: *Aurora*
1609   Shakespeare: *Sonnets*
1633   Greville: *Caelica*
1634   Habington: *Castara*

This may indicate, as Prince thinks, 'something of the air of a poetical debauch', or it may be evidence that the sonnet is (according to Matthews) 'a highly neurotic art-form' reflecting a basic antithesis between sanctified institution and passion. The sociological relevance of a verse-form is something hard to establish, but the convention of adoring the inaccessible seems to have been appropriate to the tensions of the Renaissance Court, and to have prepared the way for a genuine neo-platonism. From Sidney (lover of a 'star') to Habington (lover of a 'chaste altar') the 'donna angelicata' aspect of the beloved has encouraged an idealism of the sort that led Byron (*Journals*, 17–18 December 1813) to remark: 'They are the most puling, petrifying, stupidly platonic compositions'. In fact, the philosophical turn, which the somewhat logical structure of the English sonnet induces, is very often the saving grace of these sonnets, for as the plentiful examples of anti-Petrarchanism (such as Shakespeare 130) show, the hopes and the conventions bequeathed to the Elizabethans had a limited life. (The reader will, however, wish to pursue his study of the literary habits of the Elizabethan sonneteers in the admirable works of Scott, Lever and John.) Shakespeare himself, for instance, while recounting a situation and his feelings about it, offers from the point of view of the poetry itself a much larger perspective drawn from his understanding of human mutability. His sonnets form, to that extent, a philosophical poem. Chapman's 'A Coronet for his Mistresse Philosophie' celebrates not a girl but an idea, and one that none the less represented to the Elizabethans the highest beauty and virtue. The kind of symbolism afforded here comes quite close to what I believe is the most serious and interesting role of the sonnet sequence as an intermittent but powerfully penetrating metaphysical disquisition. The best modern examples are perhaps Rilke's *Sonette an Orpheus* and Auden's 'The Quest'. Thus the biographical element in Elizabethan sequences may be seen as the distracting gossip that it essentially is, and the Victorian's concern to establish, say, the identity of Mr W. H. (Southampton? A boy-actor? Queen Elizabeth?) as an overplayed side-issue.

Far more instructive to the reader who is conscious of the gravitation of Shakespeare's sonnets towards the philosophical problems of time is Alastair Fowler's analysis of their possible structural symbolism. He finds a monumental intention in a pyramidal form (cf. Shakespeare 123, and Milton's 'On Shakespeare') on a base of seventeen (such a pyramid yields the number 153, the number of the *Sonnets* if number 136 is removed on internal grounds). Again, Dunlop shows us how Spenser makes a structural use of the 'subject' of his courtship of Elizabeth Boyle in *Amoretti* by applying a calendrical correspondence so that it becomes 'a cycle with symmetrical beginning and end sections of twenty-one sonnets each, and a central group of forty-seven sonnets in which each sonnet corresponds to a date in Lent of 1594'. The Christian symbolism is obvious: Spenser is writing of the progression of earthly love to higher love with the transition marked by Easter. Similar numerological analyses have been made of the sequences of Daniel (see Williamson) and Sidney (see Fowler).

What we have here is one way of imposing a meaningful structure on a possibly open-ended form. If Sidney loves Penelope Rich in the guise of Astrophil loving Stella, then *Astrophil and Stella* may as well be limited to a total of 108 sonnets (the number of Penelope's suitors in Homer). Numerological symbolism is particularly appropriate to a form with discrete units (when the sonnet is not, that is, used as a stanza). It soon becomes clear, moreover, that the Elizabethan habit of interlacing sonnets in a sequence with ballads, canzonets and other lyrics can become more than a mere desire for variety; it can assist the formal structure (the stanzas of the songs in *Astrophil and Stella* also total 108). Since I am largely concerned with sonnet technique in this book, such devices attain a relevance here which perhaps in a larger poetic context they might not have, at least in relation to internal characteristics such as astronomical conceits; goddess, bird or mirror imagery; or topics such as sleeplessness and the irresponsibility of Cupid, all of which may be freely found in poems other than sonnets.

For this reason the kind of sequence known as the corona or crown of sonnets has a particular interest, since it links the units of the sequence very closely in both theme and rhyme. Actually, there are several sorts of sequence comprised under this heading. First of all, simple links can be provided by rhyme alone, as in Petrarch 41–3, each of which employ identical rhyme sounds, or as in Luigi Grotto's *Rime* in which the tercet rhymes continue in following quatrains. In a corona proper, the sonnets are linked through repetition of whole lines. In the simplest form, the last line of one sonnet becomes the first line of the next, until in the final sonnet we return in the last line to the first line of the whole sequence. Usually some simple subject demanding a limited number of sonnets is required. It should be noted that sequences of this kind (but not linked in corona) are quite common in Italian. There are the seven sonnets on the deadly sins by Fazio degli Uberti, for instance, or the sequences on the days of the week and on the months of the year by Folgore da san Gemignano (which may be read in Rossetti's translation, *Works*, 1911, pp. 465 ff). An example of such a sequence in corona would be Benedetto dell'Uva Monaco's 'Questa ghirlanda di fioretti e fronde' (1585) where the circular form of the sequence appropriately symbolizes the garland of flowers which is its subject.

Such a form is eminently suitable for elevated subjects, whether devotional (as in Donne's 'La Corona') or panegyric (as in Sylvester's 'Corona Dedicatoria' to his translation of Du Bartas). The repeated lines produce an effect of sustained lyrical statement, grand and sonorous. Donne's sequence is made up of seven (largely Sidneyan) sonnets on the life of Christ (Advent, Annunciation, Nativitie, Temple, Crucyfying, Resurrection, Ascension) in which, naturally, much play is made with the notion of crowns (the poet wishes, for instance, for thorns rather than bays, and Christ himself 'crowns' man's ends as in Isaiah 28.5: 'In that day shall the Lord of hosts be for a crown of glory, and for a diadem of beauty, unto the residue of his people'). As a prosodic device, this suits very well a poem which was, as Helen Gardner says in her edition of the *Divine Poems* (1962, p. xxii), 'inspired by liturgical prayer and praise – oral prayer; not . . . private meditation'. The tone is assisted in its solemnity and sense of inevitability by the repetitions. When cleverly varied in syntax the link-lines do double work in the sequence, as flexible hinges. Look, for instance, at this transition from the fifth to the sixth sonnet in 'La Corona', where the metamorphosis of the link-line's verb from an imperative into a participle silently anticipates the desired redemption, brings it (though still in the imagination) one stage nearer:

> Now thou art lifted up, draw mee to thee,
> And at thy death giving such liberall dole,
> *Moyst, with one drop of thy blood, my dry soule.*
>
> 6   Resurrection
> *Moyst with one drop of thy blood, my dry soule*
> Shall (though she now be in extreme degree
> Too stony hard, and yet too fleshly), bee
> Freed by that drop. . . .

Sylvester's 'Corona Dedicatoria' (*Works*, 1641, sigs. A2-A4ᵛ) contains eleven sonnets on Urania and the nine Muses (ten of them linked in corona). The interest of this sequence lies in its excessive formality, since the sonnets are arranged typographically as pillars, thus providing a third level of symbolism.

Under the s   dow of Your Sacred Boughes,
Great, Rc all CEDAR of Mount LIBANON
(Greater than that great Tree of BABYLON)
No marvaile if our TURTLE seek to house;

Sith CESAR'S Eagles, that so strongly Rouze:
Th'old Haggard FALCON, hatcht by *Pampelon:*

Th' IBERIAN GRIPHIN
(And not THESE alone,

P O L Y M N I A

But every Bird and Beast)
With HUMBLE vowes,

Seeks roost or rest under your mighty Bowers:
So mighty hath the Almigh y made you now:

O *Honour Him who thus hath Honour'd you,*
And build His house who thus hath blessed Yours,
So STUARTS ay shall stand (propt by his power)
To Foes a Terrour, and to Friends a Tower.

D

This kind of thing is the *ne plus ultra* of decorative panegyric, and is something the sonnet does well. Sylvester, incidentally, wrote a number of sonnets containing ingenious acrostics and anagrams, though this does not seem to me by any means to be an essential aspect of sonneteering. Chapman's 'A Coronet for his Mistresse Philosophie' contains ten English sonnets and was once thought to be an attack on Shakespeare as a sensual poet. The corona form assists Chapman's tone here, which is admonitory and somewhat obscure, and the subject could be said to be a devotional one, if secular.

It is clear that a corona of this kind need not be of any particular length, even though some writers expect it to contain seven sonnets. Crescimbeni, p. 213, mentions a collection of *corone* published in Padua in 1581 in which all the examples contain nine sonnets. The subject itself should dictate the length. The form is still quite popular, particularly in German. The Austrian poet Josef Weinheber, for instance, published two in *Spate Krone* (1936) and one in *Adel und Untergang* (1937).

Precise length is dictated by a more elaborate kind of corona described by Crescimbeni (p. 214) in which fourteen sonnets are linked in the usual manner and a fifteenth added in which all the link-lines appear in order. This form, sometimes called the *sonnet redoublé*, can be arranged in more than one way. The fifteenth sonnet (the *sonetto magistrale*) could, for instance, come at the beginning. It will be realized that if the Italian sonnet is used (as it should be) a certain virtuosity in rhyming will be called for, since the *sonetto magistrale*'s rhymes will crop up insistently throughout the sequence and the poet must find twenty-four each of its two octave rhymes and twelve each of its three sestet rhymes (if a type 1 sestet is used). An example given by Crescimbeni is his own 'Ghirlanda di fronde, e fiore' where Lucrina is decked in fourteen of the sonnets with fourteen different flowers, each symbolizing one of her qualities. Some modern poets have also tackled this form (see Agnes Gergely, *Johanna*, Budapest, 1968; George MacBeth, 'A Christmas Ring' in *The Burning Cone*, London, 1970; and John Fuller, *The Labours of Hercules*, Manchester, 1970).

As if this were not enough, Crescimbeni produced in collaboration a triple corona of this sort, containing forty sonnets, called 'Corona rinterzata' (Crescimbeni, pp. 214–15). In it, the lines of the *sonetto magistrale* are deployed in the sequence in order, then alternately from the middle outwards, and then in reverse order. The subject of this Arcadian extravaganza was the pontification of Clement XI, and Crescimbeni was delighted to point out that it was so titled 'perchè in verità ella è Corona tre volte replicata' (alluding to the tiara or triple crown of the Pope). With such symbolism does this baroque form attain the height of symbolic propriety.

The development of the narrative sequence is of some interest, for it is a development which seems to have come to fruition in the nineteenth century, when the sonnet sequence again attained some popularity. Such narrative sequences as Cadurcis's in Disraeli's *Venetia* (1837) cannot have had much influence, but by the 1860s a number of Victorian poets were clothing autobiographical material in fictional dress. Meredith's 'Modern Love' (1862), Hardy's 'She, to Him' (1866) and George Eliot's 'Brother and Sister' (1869) all relate very closely to the experience of their authors, but, like Mrs Browning in her 'Sonnets from the Portuguese' (1850), they preferred to appear at a distance from this experience. Hardy, for instance, gives the voice in his very brief sequence to (possibly) Tryphaena Sparks, something that would have been unthinkable to an Elizabethan. Indeed, it was the passion of the 'Sonnets from the Portuguese' that made it seem difficult for Mrs Browning to offer them *in propria persona*.

Meredith's sequence, though in sixteen-line poems (abbacddceffeghhg), is a triumph of psychological realism. Its

confessional element has been overstressed, and if we trace
Meredith's guilt about his wife who ran away with a painter, was
deserted by him and died alone, we tend to miss the novelist's
creative insights into the confused and deceptive textures of a
stale marriage. It perhaps would not be denied that the plot of the
sequence (the wife poisons herself so that the hero may go to his
new love) wears a melodramatic air; but the poem's path through
its obliquely related incidents is so memorable in its insistent
probing of the couple's weaknesses and misunderstandings, that it
finally succeeds in the same sort of way that any good amatory
sequence succeeds – by the repeated lyrical exposure of a self-
conscious sensibility in units which progress by collision and
juxtaposition.

The temptation to call such a work a 'poem' rather than a
'sequence' underlines the dangers to the sonnet's identity in its
purely narrative role. When a work like Wilfrid Blunt's 'Esther'
(1892) quickens its narrative pace, the form of the individual
sonnet blurs noticeably, and in cases where the sonnet is being
used largely as a mere stanza (as in, for instance, the 209 sonnets
of William Ellery Leonard's ambitious *Two Lives*, 1926), for
much of the time one wonders why the sonnet was chosen at all.
However, the narrative mode can certainly provide dynamic
images for the poet. One thinks of John Crowe Ransom's 'Two
Gentlemen in Bonds' (*Selected Poems*, 1970, pp. 95–106) with the
delicate balance of its cddeec sestet. Ransom's sequence is however
quirky and allegorical, and narrative is hardly its main point.

Where a sequence is less the poetic equivalent of a novel than
a short story (as in, for instance, Edna St Vincent Millay's 'Sonnets
from an Ungrafted Tree', *Collected Poems*, New York, 1956, pp.
606–22), true narrative success is possible and a success, moreover,
peculiar to the form. This sequence is preferable to her more
celebrated 'Fatal Interview' (ibid., pp. 630–81) because the latter is
too consciously Elizabethan in mode, as is perhaps Rossetti's 'The

House of Life' (1863–81). The attitudes of the Elizabethans remain powerful models, and are the natural starting point for John Berryman (*Berryman's Sonnets*, 1968) or for the satirical anti-Petrarchanism of something like Christopher Caudwell's 'Twenty Sonnets of Wm Smith' (*Poems*, 1965, pp. 26–36). William Smith, a real Elizabethan, would have found the tribute a little cynical, but he might have approved the energetic scorn.

In the modern period the sonnet sequence has been found suitable for more meditative or speculative treatment of public themes. As with the love sequence, mere accumulation of material (particularly over a period of time) does not give unity to a number of sonnets gathered together. Re-ordering of material to give greater coherence is a favourite scholarly activity, though it is not clear that, say, Milton's sonnets gain from this. Nor is it clear that Shakespeare's do, despite circumstances of publication. In historical or political subjects, arrangement may be either diachronistic or synchronistic. The youthful Jacobinism of Coleridge's 'Sonnets on Eminent Characters' is the only justification of the series, which is thus closely bound in time and attitude. Wordsworth's 132 'Ecclesiastical Sonnets' on the other hand, though just as pregnant with opinion and polemic, form an historical study of an institution, implying a more comprehensive, less selective series, and disguising to some extent the Anglican apologetics.

Into the class of sequences on particular occasions fall such works as Blunt's 'In Vinculis' (1888) or Lowell's *Notebook* (rev. 1970), though the latter's terms of reference are so broad that the comparatively narrow period of time covered by the sequence seems to offer very little limitation of subject. Lowell calls *Notebook* a poem, moreover, rather than a sequence, but here one imagines that he merely wishes to deny the particular discreteness for so long presumed to be characteristic of short poems in modern collections.

Auden's 'Sonnets from China' (1937) begins as a diachronistic sequence, encompassing in symbolic terms the whole history of man since Eden, but turns sharply midway to an examination of the particular circumstances of the Sino-Japanese war. Roy Fuller's 'Mythological Sonnets' (*Collected Poems*, 1969, pp. 201–10) have no chronological implications, but like Auden's 'The Quest' (1941) derive from Rilke the method of assembling archetypal symbols and incidents for the purpose of examining aspects of the human situation. Rilke's imagery (Orpheus, the rose, children playing) involved the spirituality of art, Auden's (the fairy-tale world of the quest) the individual's spiritual destiny, and Fuller's (the world of fable and metamorphosis) the individual's psycho-sexual inheritance. In sequences like these, and to a certain extent in Dylan Thomas's rather brashly religious 'Altarwise by Owl-light' (1936), a wealth of difficult perception on numinous, metaphysical and psychological subjects found itself capable of expression in abrupt, allusive, pictorial and even obliquely narrative terms.

History itself is still a possible subject for the sequence as James Fenton's *Our Western Furniture* (Oxford, 1968) shows. This ironic examination of the confrontation of East and West at the time of Perry's opening of Japan uses its ingenious symmetrical arrangement of three groups of seven sonnets as a conscious means of historical and dramatic organization. In part 1 the Japanese anticipate, and in part 3 the Americans reminisce. In part 2 they meet, and in the central sonnet of the sequence display their skills (abcdefggfedcba). In company with an ingenious use of personae, such a device becomes pointed and meaningful, and is a reminder of the wealth of structural possibilities inherent in the very notion of the sonnet sequence, and still largely unexplored.

One poet evidently keen to confront these possibilities head-on is Jacques Roubaud. His ∈ (Paris, 1967) is composed of 361 'texts' described as 'sonnets, sonnets courts, sonnets interrompus, sonnets en prose, sonnets courts en prose, citations, illustrations, grilles, blancs, noirs, poèmes, poèmes en prose . . .' and the whole work may be read in four quite different ways, one of which follows the procedures of a Japanese game of Go (a plan of the game is provided). Another aspect of the structure may be seen in Roubaud's claim that he forms what I suppose could be described as meta-sonnets, since each sonnet is given an identity as either a black or white piece in Go, and therefore a series of such black or white sonnets may be arranged as follows (as are the first fourteen in the sequence): ○ ● ○ ● (blanc) ● ○ ● ○ (blanc) ○ ● ○ (blanc) ○ ● ○, forming a 'sonnet de sonnets'.

With such sophistications of the form to be considered it would seem that we have moved a long way from the basic point of the sonnet as I described it in my first chapter. Some critics (like William Carlos Williams in an afterword to Merrill Moore's *M*, New York, 1938) feel that the sonnet has not moved far enough; others (like Pound, *Literary Essays*, London, 1954, pp. 170–1) that it has moved too far, indeed has been somewhat vitiated since it was sundered from its musical setting in about 1290. We have no need to take sides in a disagreement of that kind. The sonnet is alive and possible.

Bibliography

This selected list of further reading is arranged in alphabetical order. It includes the works referred to in the text by surname of author.

ATTENBOROUGH, G. M., 'The Sonnet from Milton to Wordsworth', *Gentleman's Magazine*, CCXCII (1902).

BALDI, SERGIO, *La Poesia di Wyatt*, Florence, 1953.

BATESON, F. W., *English Poetry: a Critical Introduction*, London, 1950. Chap. 6: 'Sir Thomas Wyatt and the Renaissance' contains an interesting comparison between 'Whoso lists to hunt, I know where is an hind' and Petrarch 157.

BULLITT, J. M., 'The Use of Rhyme Link in the Sonnets of Sidney, Drayton and Spenser', *Journal of English and Germanic Philology*, XLIX (1950).

BULLOCK, W. L., 'The Genesis of the English Sonnet Form', *PMLA*, XXXVIII (1923). This is a particularly useful article.

CRESCIMBENI, GIOVAN MARIO DE, *L'Istoria della Volgar Poesia*, Venice, 1730–1. This is a pioneering work of literary history by one of the founders of the Arcadia. Vol. I, Book III, chap. 9: 'Delle Corone, e altra spezie di più Sonetti legati insieme' is of particular value.

CROSLAND, T. W. H., *The English Sonnet*, New York, 1917. This critic takes the orthodoxy of the Italian sonnet to unnecessary extremes.

DENNIS, JOHN, 'The English Sonnet' in *Studies in English Literature* London 1876.

DUNLOP, ALEXANDER, 'The Unity of Spenser's Amoretti' in Alastair Fowler, ed., *Silent Poetry*, London, 1970. An interesting calendrical analysis.

EQUICOLA, MARIO, *Institutioni al comporre in ogni sorte di Rima*, Milan, 1536.

FOWLER, ALASTAIR, *Triumphal Forms*, Cambridge, 1970. Chap. 9: 'Sonnet Sequences' is a fascinating investigation of certain numerological structures in Elizabethan sequences.

FUSSELL, PAUL, JR., *Poetic Meter and Poetic Form*, New York, 1965. Chap. 6: 'Structural Principles: the example of the Sonnet'. It is hard to think of a more lively or suggestive introduction to prosody, so that this chapter is of central importance.

GARDNER, W. H., *Gerard Manley Hopkins* (revised), London, 1948. Chap. 3: 'Sonnet Morphology'.

HAMER, E., *The English Sonnet*, London, 1936. An anthology (up to Rupert Brooke only) with a sensible introduction.

HAVENS, R. D., *The Influence of Milton on English Poetry* (revised), Boston, Mass., 1961. This is the basic authority for the sonnet in the eighteenth century.

HUNT, LEIGH, and LEE, S. A., eds., *The Book of the Sonnet*, Boston, Mass., 1867.

JOHN, LISLE CECIL, *Elizabethan Sonnet Sequences*, New York, 1938. Useful for its tabulation of Elizabethan sonnet motifs.

KASTNER, L. E., 'Concerning the Sonnet of the Sonnet', *Modern Language Review*, XI (1916). This article traces about a dozen examples of the kind of sonnet which is itself about the problems of writing a sonnet.

LEVER, J. W., *The Elizabethan Love Sonnet*, London, 1956. The best book on the subject.

LOFFT, CAPEL, *Laura, or an anthology of sonnets on the Petrarcan model*, 1814, 5 vols.

MCKILLOP, A. D., 'Some details of the Sonnet Revival', *Modern Language Notes*, XXXIX (1924). A useful supplement to Havens.

MAIN, DAVID M., *A Treasury of English Sonnets*, Manchester, 1880.

MATTHEWS, G. M., 'Sex and the Sonnet', *Essays in Criticism*, II (1952). With a reply by P. N. Siegel.

MÖNCH, W., *Das Sonett, Gestalt und Geschichte*, Heidelberg, 1955. This is the best study of the sonnet, and gives a comprehensive view of its development throughout Europe.

MORTON, E. P., 'The English Sonnet (1658–1750)', *Modern Language Notes*, XX (1905).

PRAZ, MARIO, 'Petrarch in England' in *The Flaming Heart*, New York, 1958.

PRINCE, F. T., 'The Sonnet from Wyatt to Shakespeare' in *Elizabethan Poetry*, Stratford-upon-Avon Studies 2, 1960.

RAJNA, PIO, 'Come nacque il sonetto', *Il Marzocco* (25 May 1924).

RINAKER, C., 'Thomas Edwards and the Sonnet Revival', *Modern Language Notes*, XXXIV (1919).

RUSSELL, REV. MATTHEW, S. J., *Sonnets on the Sonnet: an Anthology*, London, 1898.

SAINTSBURY, GEORGE, *A History of English Prosody*, London, 1906.

SANDERLIN, G., 'The Influence of Milton and Wordsworth on the Early Victorian Sonnet', *English Literary History*, V (1938).

SCOTT, JANET G., *Les Sonnets Elisabéthains*, Paris, 1929. Particularly useful for the minor sonneteers.

SHARP, WILLIAM, ed., *Sonnets of this Century*, London, 1888.

SIEGEL, P. N., 'The Petrarchan Sonneteers and Neo-Platonic Love', *Studies in Philology*, XLII (1945). Contrasts the 'Petrarchan' attitude of the old nobility with the 'Neo-Platonic' attitude of the new aristocracy.

STERNER, G., *The Sonnet in American Literature*, University of Pennsylvania, 1930.

TEMPO, ANTONIO DA, *Summa artis rithimici*, 1332. Published Venice, 1509. Early account of the sonnet noting sixteen different varieties.

TOMLINSON, C., *The Sonnet: its Origin, Structure and Place in Poetry*, London, 1874.

TRISSINO, GIOVANNI GIORGIO, *Poetica*, Vicenza, 1529.

WILKINS, E. H., *Studies in Italian Literature*, Rome, 1959. The authority on the origin of the sonnet.

WILLIAMSON, C. F., 'The Design of Daniel's *Delia*', *Review of English Studies*, ns XIX (1968).

Index